READING CORNER

Ellie's Star

Written by
Jillian Powell

Illustrated by
Elisa Squillace

W
FRANKLIN WATTS
LONDON•SYDNEY

Jillian Powell

"Stars are among my favourite things. I don't think there's anything more magical than looking at a starry night sky."

Elisa Squillace

"I live in a little town on the shore of the beautiful Lake Maggiore in the north of Italy. I can see lots of stars over the lake at night."

Every day, Ellie's teacher
gave out a gold star.

On Monday, it was for being quiet in story-time. Ellie sat very quietly.

CINDERELLA

7

Then Daniel pulled Ellie's ponytail.

"OUCH!" Ellie squealed loudly.

On Tuesday, Ellie's teacher
was giving a gold star for
handwriting. Ellie wrote
her name very carefully.

Then SPLODGE went the ink.

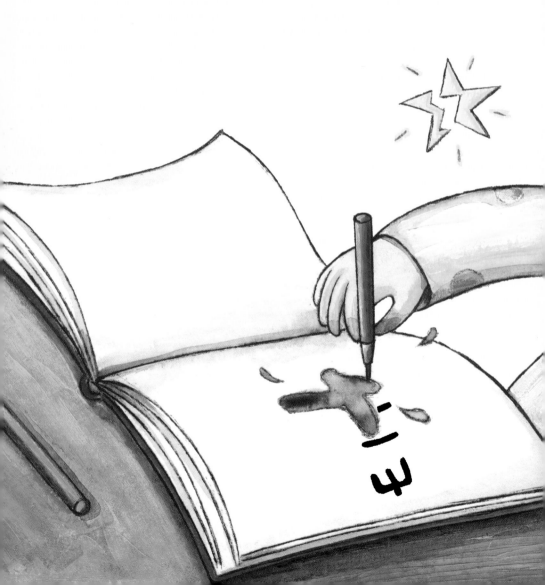

13

On Wednesday, Ellie's teacher was giving a gold star for a tidy desk. Ellie kept her desk very tidy.

15

Then CRASH went the books.

1+1=2
2+2=4
3+3=6
4+4=8
5+5=10

A B
G H
P

"Never mind," said Dad when Ellie told him. "You'll get a gold star soon!"

On Thursday, Ellie's teacher was giving a gold star for painting.

Ellie painted a lovely picture.

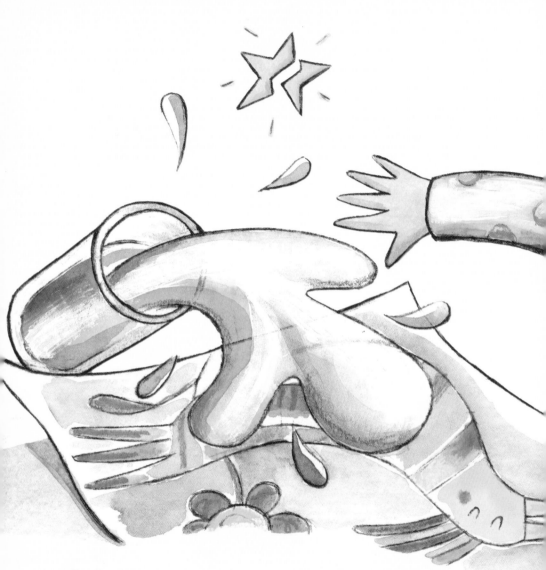

Then SPLASH went the water.

"I'll never get a gold star!"
Ellie told Dad.

"Don't be silly, Ellie," Dad said.
"Don't you know? Everyone has
a star. Come and see Ellie's star!"

Dad showed Ellie her star.

On Friday, Ellie wrote a poem about her star.

And Ellie's teacher gave her ...

... a gold star!

Notes for parents and teachers

READING CORNER has been structured to provide maximum support for new readers. The stories may be used by adults for sharing with young children. Primarily, however, the stories are designed for newly independent readers, whether they are reading these books in bed at night, or in the reading corner at school or in the library.

Starting to read alone can be a daunting prospect. READING CORNER helps by providing visual support and repeating words and phrases, while making reading enjoyable. These books will develop confidence in the new reader, and encourage a love of reading that will last a lifetime!

If you are reading this book with a child, here are a few tips:

1. Make reading fun! Choose a time to read when you and the child are relaxed and have time to share the story.

2. Encourage children to reread the story, and to retell the story in their own words, using the illustrations to remind them what has happened.

3. Give praise! Remember that small mistakes need not always be corrected.

READING CORNER covers three grades of early reading ability, with three levels at each grade. Each level has a certain number of words per story, indicated by the number of bars on the spine of the book, to allow you to choose the right book for a young reader:

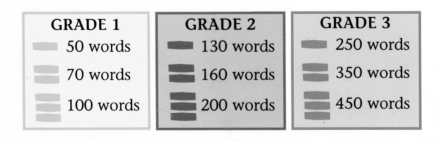

GRADE 1	GRADE 2	GRADE 3
50 words	130 words	250 words
70 words	160 words	350 words
100 words	200 words	450 words